W9-BUM-648

STREP THROAT

ELAINE LANDAU

Marshall Cavendish
Benchmark
New York

Expert Reader: Dr. Stuart E. Beeber of Chappaqua Pediatrics, Chappaqua, New York

Published by Marshall Cavendish Benchmark
An imprint of Marshall Cavendish Corporation

Website: www.marshallcavendish.us

This publication represents the opinions and views of the author based on Elaine Landau's personal experience, knowledge, and research. The information in this book serves as a general guide only. The author and publisher have used their best efforts in preparing this book and disclaim liability rising directly and indirectly from the use and application of this book.

Other Marshall Cavendish Offices:
Marshall Cavendish International (Asia) Private Limited, 1 New Industrial Road, Singapore 536196 • Marshall Cavendish International (Thailand) Co Ltd. 253 Asoke, 12th Flr, Sukhumvit 21 Road, Klongtoey Nua, Wattana, Bangkok 10110, Thailand • Marshall Cavendish (Malaysia) Sdn Bhd, Times Subang, Lot 46, Subang Hi-Tech Industrial Park, Batu Tiga, 40000 Shah Alam, Selangor Darul Ehsan, Malaysia

Marshall Cavendish is a trademark of Times Publishing Limited

All websites were available and accurate when this book was sent to press.

Library of Congress Cataloging-in-Publication Data

Landau, Elaine.
Strep throat / by Elaine Landau.
p. cm. — (Head-to-toe health)
Includes index.
Summary: "Provides basic information about strep throat and its prevention"—Provided by publisher.
    ISBN 978-0-7614-4834-1
    1. Streptococcal infections—Juvenile literature. 2. Throat—Diseases—Juvenile literature. I. Title.
    RC116.S84.L365 2010
    616.9'298—dc22
    2009030837

Editor: Joy Bean
Publisher: Michelle Bisson
Art Director: Anahid Hamparian
Series Designer: Alex Ferrari

Photo research by Candlepants Incorporated

Cover Photo: Doctor Stock/Science Faction / Corbis

The photographs in this book are used by permission and through the courtesy of: *Shutterstock*: 4. *Getty Images*: Steven Peters, 7; Jeffrey Coolidge, 9; Dr. David Phillips, 11; E. Dygas, 14; Gabrielle Revere, 16; Tim Platt, 17; Peter Dazeley, 19; Mimi Haddon, 24; DK Stock/Robert Glenn, 26. *Alamy Images*: Scott Camazine, 12; Jack Sullivan, 22. *Corbis*: Lester V. Bergman, 20.

Printed in Malaysia (T).

1 3 5 6 4 2

CONTENTS

FEELING YUCKY

You're sick. You knew it the minute you got up this morning. You had a bad sore throat.

You felt miserable for the rest of the day, too. You lost your appetite. You didn't want to eat even after your mom made your favorite lunch—spaghetti and meatballs.

By evening, you couldn't imagine eating anything. At that point, your throat hurt badly. It felt raw and sore. It was getting very hard to swallow. You could hardly get down a few sips of water.

That wasn't all. Your stomach hurt, and you felt really hot. Your mother took your temperature, and you had a fever.

You opened your mouth wide to get a good look at your throat in the mirror. You didn't like what you saw. It looked pretty yucky in there. Your throat was very red, and there were white patches of **pus** at the back.

◀ This girl has a sore throat and it is hard for her to swallow. She may have strep throat.

Your mother felt the **glands** in your neck. They felt sore when she touched them. You weren't surprised when your mother told you that your glands were swollen. Your mother didn't sound surprised either when she said, "You may have strep throat. Looks like you'll need to see the doctor."

Anyone can get strep throat. Yet it is especially common in kids from ages five to fifteen. That includes you and a lot of your friends.

This is a book about strep throat. You'll find out what to do if you get strep throat. You'll also learn ways to lessen your chances of getting it. So start reading—and staying healthy.

UNFAIR TO YOUNG FOLKS

Who said germs are fair? They aren't. Strep throat is a perfect example. Adults who get strep throat tend to have milder **symptoms** than kids and teens. In some cases, adults may not even know they have strep throat.

Here a doctor examines his young patient's glands. Swollen glands can be a sign of strep throat.

WHAT IS STREP THROAT?

Do you think you can hide from germs? Think again. Germs are everywhere on the planet. You couldn't find a germ-free zone to live in if you tried.

There are different types of germs, too. Two kinds of germs that can cause sore throats are **viruses** and bacteria.

MORE ABOUT GERMS

Viruses can't live on their own for very long. They need to be inside a living thing, like a human, to survive. Someone like you would do just fine. Once a virus gets inside your body, it thrives and multiplies.

Viruses are really small. It doesn't matter if you have perfect vision. You can't see them with the naked eye.

GOOD GUYS VERSUS BAD GUYS

You don't want to get near the bacteria
that cause strep throat. But not all bacteria are bad.
Some bacteria in our bodies help us digest our food.
Other bacteria are used in making foods. Some bacteria
make milk go sour. These bacteria are used to make
cottage cheese, buttermilk, and yogurt.

To see them, you need a special tool called an **electron microscope**.

It's hard to picture something smaller than a virus. They are among the tiniest germs on Earth. More than 300 billion viruses can fit on the period at the end of this sentence.

Even though they are small, viruses can make you feel super miserable. These germs cause the common cold, the flu, chicken pox, and lots of other illnesses.

Viruses can also give you a sore throat. That's often the first sign of a cold. Usually this sore throat will go away on its own after a few days. It's not strep throat.

A virus cannot cause strep throat—bacteria do that. Bacteria are small, one-celled organisms. Some bacteria are germs. They are tiny, but they are bigger than viruses. Only about a million bacteria could fit on the period at the end of this sentence. Unlike viruses, bacteria can reproduce, or multiply, inside or outside a living being.

When certain bacteria enter your body, they can cause ear infections, cavities, **pneumonia**, and other illnesses. The bacterium that causes strep throat is known as group A streptococcus. That's a big name for a tiny, egg-shaped germ. It's called GAS for short.

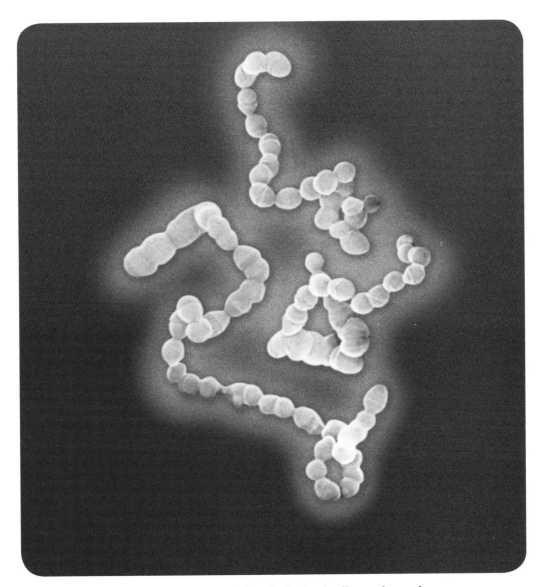

This is how a chain of strep throat bacteria looks through a microscope.

SIGNS OF STREP THROAT

If you get strep throat, you won't have the same symptoms as a common cold. Your sore throat will probably feel a lot worse than the sore throat you would get with a cold. You'll also often have a fever, swollen glands, nausea, and a loss of appetite. Your throat will probably look very red, with white patches at the back and on your tonsils. In some cases, you might also get a skin rash. This rash most often appears all over the body, but it is darker in the armpit and groin areas.

GET TO A DOCTOR

Most people don't go to the doctor when they have a cold. A cold usually clears up on its own. But it's different with strep throat. It is important to see a doctor. In very rare cases, if left untreated, strep throat can lead to more serious health problems.

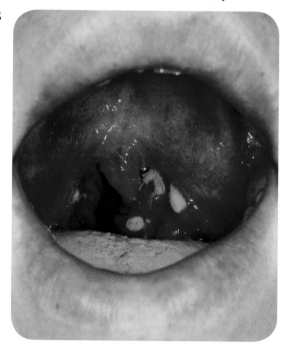

Notice the white patches at the back of this child's throat. These are a symptom of strep throat.

From Kid to Kid

Some things should spread easily. You want butter to spread smoothly across your toast. The same goes for icing on a birthday cake or jelly on a peanut butter sandwich.

No one wants strep throat to spread, yet this illness can spread very easily. Do you know how strep throat spreads? Take this quick quiz to see.

SCENE 1

A boy in your class has strep throat, but he doesn't know it yet. He was coughing this morning, and he didn't cover his mouth. Luckily, you don't sit next to him. Your desk is in the row in front of his. That means you're safe. True or false?

SCENE 2

You're learning a new game in gym class. The game starts with everybody holding hands in a large circle. The kid next to you has strep throat and hasn't washed his hands all

Can you get strep throat while playing a game at school? Take the quiz on pages 13 and 14 to find out.

morning. But you're okay because you only held hands with him for a minute. True or false?

SCENE 3

It's a hot day, and you and your best friend are at the playground. Both of you are thirsty, but you only have enough money for one soda. So you share a soda. The next day, your friend comes down with strep throat. You're sure that you'll stay well, though. Your friend's symptoms don't show up until the next morning. That means you're out of danger. True or false?

In each of these three scenes, the answer is false. You could easily get strep throat in any of these situations. Strep throat is passed from infected people to healthy people. GAS bacteria are carried in **mucus** and other bodily fluids. If a person with strep throat sneezes or coughs, the germs spread through the air. When this happens, all you have to do is breathe to become infected.

DO YOU KNOW THE ANSWER?

How soon do strep throat symptoms usually appear after someone has been exposed to the illness?

A. several hours

B. seven to ten days

C. two to five days

The correct answer is C, two to five days. This is known as the **incubation period**—the amount of time before you start feeling sick.

LOTS OF WAYS TO GET INFECTED

To catch strep throat, you don't even have to be in the same room as the infected person. Let's say an infected person sneezes, and the **airborne** droplets land on a doorknob.

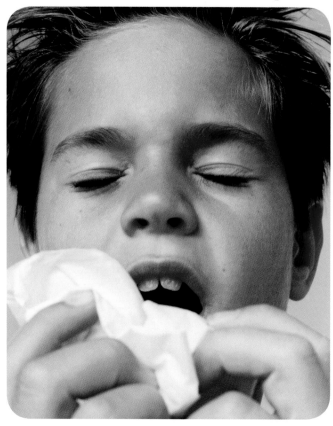

You should always cover your mouth when you sneeze. This will help prevent other people from coming in contact with your germs.

You're the next person to open the door. Now the germs are on your hands, but you don't know it. Minutes later you touch your face, which means you bring the germs near your nose and mouth. Guess what? Now you may be infected.

Still another way to get infected is by sharing food or silverware. You finish off your little sister's ice cream sundae with the same spoon she used. Later on, her throat starts to hurt. The next day, you learn that she has strep throat. She might not be the only one in the family. You could be next!

The number of strep throat cases is especially high in the late fall and winter. Large groups of students are together in classrooms and crowded hallways. The GAS bacteria land on pencils, books, and desks that lots of kids use. Strep throat can easily spread through a class.

But that's not all. The infected children go home after school. There they can infect their brothers, sisters, and other family members. Picture this happening in many homes. That's how strep throat can spread through a town.

Strep throat has been known to spread through schools.

It Happened to You

You hoped you wouldn't get strep throat. It was the last thing you wanted to happen. But lots of kids at school have it. And now you have all the symptoms, too. Is there any hope for you?

Sure there is! You're going to be just fine. But to make sure that happens, you've got to see your doctor. You should never ignore the symptoms of strep throat—especially if you have a fever.

AT THE DOCTOR'S OFFICE

Don't be nervous about seeing the doctor for strep throat. Nothing painful will happen to you. You'll just be starting down the road to getting better.

The doctor will ask you questions about your symptoms. You'll need to be examined, too. Your doctor has to get a good look at your throat. It's important to be sure that you have strep throat and not a common cold.

TESTING, TESTING...

Usually your doctor will give you a test called a rapid strep test. This is a quick and painless test. The doctor uses a special swab to take a sample of the cells at the back of your throat. It takes only a few minutes to test the cells.

If the test results are positive, it means you have strep throat. That may not sound very positive to you, but look at the bright side. Once the doctor is sure you have strep throat, you can be treated for it.

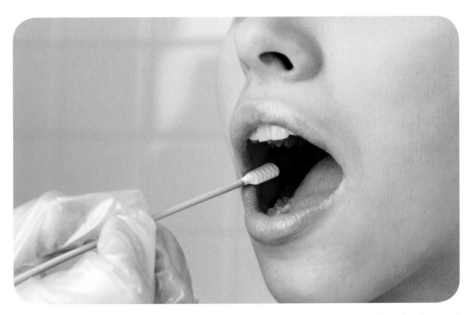

In this picture a doctor takes a sample of cells from the back of an ill child's throat to test for strep throat.

But what if your rapid strep test comes back negative? Does that mean you don't have strep throat after all? Maybe or maybe not. Rapid strep tests give correct results about 75 to 85 percent of the time. Sometimes these tests give false negatives. That means that you really have strep throat even though the test says you don't.

So what if the doctor still thinks you have strep throat? Then he or she will take a throat culture. With this test, your doctor uses a cotton swab to take a small sample of cells from the back of your throat. The cells are placed in a container, called a Petri dish, with a substance that helps strep bacteria grow.

If GAS bacteria grow in the dish, you have strep throat. If they don't grow, you do not have strep. It usually takes a day or two to get the results from a throat culture, but this test is more accurate than the rapid strep test.

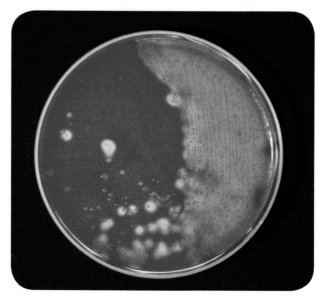

Here strep throat bacteria grow in a Petri dish.

If you have strep throat, your doctor will give you a drug called an **antibiotic**. One common antibiotic is penicillin. There are others as well. These drugs kill the bacteria that cause strep throat. They also shorten the time that you are **contagious**. After taking antibiotics for twenty-four hours, you can't give strep throat to anyone else. That means you can go back to school and be with your friends again.

Your fever will also go down in about twenty-four hours. In another couple of days, your other symptoms will disappear as well. You'll feel like your old self again. You'll have won out over those germs!

DON'T STOP TREATMENT

Be sure to finish the antibiotic you are taking for strep throat. You'll probably have to take the drug for ten days. Don't stop taking your medicine early if your symptoms improve. If you stop the medicine early, your symptoms might return.

GET TREATED!

If you have strep throat, get treated for it! Without antibiotics, you can stay contagious for weeks or even longer. You will also be at risk for other rare health problems, such as rheumatic fever—an illness that can affect your heart. Before doctors could treat strep throat with antibiotics, many children died from rheumatic fever. Today, antibiotics are widely available. The risk of developing rheumatic fever from strep throat is very low.

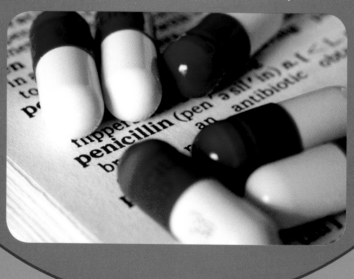

I Never Want to Get Strep Throat Again

When you have strep throat, you feel awful. You'll feel better once you're on antibiotics. But is there any help for you in the meantime?

Get ready for some good news—there is. While you're sick, try to make yourself as comfortable as possible. Many doctors give their patients more than just antibiotics. They also allow patients to take over-the-counter drugs like ibuprofen or acetaminophen. These drugs lower your fever. They also help to relieve your throat pain. You can ask your doctor if it's okay to take one of these drugs.

REST AND RELAX

This is not the time to go out and play volleyball. You can

skip gymnastics, too. Try to take it easy. Get as much rest as you can.

Don't eat hard or scratchy foods. That means passing on the potato chips. Instead, have soft foods that are easy to swallow. Soups, ice cream, and yogurt are all good choices. Also, drink plenty of fluids. Warm tea with honey and other soothing drinks can make your throat feel better.

STAYING WELL

After getting over strep throat, you want to

Soup is a good choice for lunch when you have strep throat. It is easy to swallow and won't scratch your throat.

stay well. Of course, you can't tell the germs around you to take a hike. But you can stay healthy in other ways.

Try to keep your distance from anyone who has strep throat. What if your little brother has it, and he hasn't been on antibiotics for twenty-four hours yet? Should you kiss him good night? Not a good idea. He'll know you still love him if you wait until he's better.

Wash your hands often. Don't be in a hurry to leave the sink, either. Most people wash their hands too quickly. You should be able to sing the "Happy Birthday" song twice before you finish lathering up. Always use soap and warm water when washing your hands. Be sure to dry them well, too.

Don't share food, beverages, or eating utensils with others. That doesn't make you selfish. Think about it. When you do this, you're also sharing your germs. Nobody thinks that's a great idea.

IF YOU HAVE STREP THROAT

If you have strep throat, try not to give it to your friends and family. Use tissues instead of handkerchiefs. You can throw tissues away after using them instead of carrying around germs with you. Don't share towels or bedding with your family while you're sick. Remember to cover your mouth when you cough, too.

With proper care, you'll soon be well. Do what you can to stay that way. Try to eat healthy foods, exercise, and get plenty of rest. You'll build up your body's defenses. That's a good recipe for keeping strep throat away.

Get plenty of rest, exercise, and eat healthy food. Doing those things will help you stay well.

GLOSSARY

airborne — traveling through the air

antibiotic — a drug used to kill harmful bacteria

contagious — able to be spread from one person to another

electron microscope — a microscope in which a beam of electrons creates a larger image of an object

glands — a cell, group of cells, or organ that removes materials from the body, alters them, and uses them for further use in the body

incubation period — the amount of time it takes for the signs of an illness to appear

mucus — a sticky substance produced by the body

pneumonia — a disease in which the lungs become inflamed

pus — a yellowish fluid made up of white blood cells, tissue debris, and microorganisms

symptoms — signs of an illness

viruses — tiny germs too small to be seen without a special microscope

FIND OUT MORE

BOOKS

Boudreau, Hélène. *Miraculous Medicines*. New York: Crabtree
Publications, 2009.

Glaser, Jason. *Strep Throat*. Mankato, MN: Capstone Press, 2007.

Kornberg, Arthur. *Germ Stories*. Sausalito, CA: University Science
Books, 2007.

Powell, Jillian. *Sore Throat*. North Mankato, MN: Cherrytree
Publications, 2007.

Rosenberg, Pam. *Blecch! Icky, Sticky, Gross Stuff in Your School*.
Mankato, MN: Child's World, 2008.

DVDS

All About Health & Hygiene. Schlessinger Media, 2006.

Handwashing for Kids with Soapy. Rocket88studios, 2008.

WEBSITES

The Scoop on Strep Throat

Get some quick facts on strep throat from this website, designed especially for kids.

http://kidshealth.org/PageManager.jsp?dn=KidsHealth&lic=1&ps=307&cat_id=114&article_set=22318

What Are Bacteria?

Check out this website on bacteria. You'll learn a lot about germs. Don't miss the links to all the fun games and quizzes.

http://archive.food.gov.uk/hea/711/english/part1.html

INDEX

Page numbers in **boldface** are illustrations.

ABOUT THE AUTHOR

Award-winning author Elaine Landau has written more than three hundred books for young readers. Many of them are on health and science topics.

Landau received a bachelor's degree in English and journalism from New York University and a master's degree in library and information science from Pratt Institute. You can visit her website at www.elainelandau.com.